The Book of Stones

ADAM SCHWARTZMAN was born in Johannesburg in 1973. His publications include *The Good Life. The Dirty Life. And Other Stories* (1995), *Merrie Afrika!* (1997), and *Ten South African Poets* (editor, 1999). He studied at Merton and Pembroke Colleges, Oxford, and currently lives in Pretoria, where he works in the South African National Treasury.

T0149165

ADAM SCHWARTZMAN

The Book of Stones

CARCANET

Acknowledgements

I am grateful to the following publications in which some of the poems collected in this anthology first appeared: *Carapace, New Coin, New Contrast* (South Africa); *PN Review, Poetry Review, Critical Quarterly, Stand* (UK); *The Shop* (Ireland); *Quadrant* (Australia); and to St John's College Cambridge, for the generous funding that made possible the opportunity to write many of these poems.

First published in Great Britain in 2003 by
Carcanet Press Limited
Alliance House
Cross Street
Manchester M2 7AQ

A CIP catalogue record for this book is available from the British Library
ISBN 1 85754 640 7
The publisher acknowledges financial assistance from
Arts Council England

Typeset in Monotype Bembo by XL Publishing Services, Tiverton
Printed and bound in England by SRP Ltd, Exeter

Contents

Full House Only Now

A

The birds are flying through, *A*, filling the empty houses, but only now.
Come *A*, it is full house only now.

Come *A*, the stars have dripped into the upturned jars,
and the coals blush
and the fires sting like cuts.

Come *A*, it is one moment among other moments. It is something
                                        rather than nothing,
so come –

climb into the sinews of a body,
enfold yourself between muscle and bone,
wear your skin as a suit,

but come *A*,
since how glorious now are the fisherman-seafarers and their long
                                                    canoe-barks
vibrant as taxis
and the ocean skidding over itself like sand,

and the glittery electric bodies
of delicate women,
and their soft intelligent faces concealing biology,

how glorious is the winking of the snap-eye cameras,
and the letter-writers clicking like rain,
and the pointsmen's sleeves that are blazoned with stars.

Come *A*, as soon as you can,
before the cool earth enters the soles of our feet,
before we melt through the ears of corn,
through the steel churns steaming in the dawn air,
passing invisibly,
through trellises hanging with fruit like soft balloons,
being like the air,
being less than matter,
being, like time and space, a medium, a property of existence,
as nowhere as velocity or mass,
unreal even to ourselves.

So come *A*,
be a brilliant child racing towards a calamity,
be a whore to the right touch,
be reckless and breakable,
be open to defeat,
                    but come
because this is something rather than nothing,
this takes a moment, then it goes,
this is a conversation between intimates travelling,
this takes an effort of the soul.

Come *A*, since the birds are flying through, filling the empty houses.
Come *A*, it is full house only now.

Heart of Darkness

Here is the woman I love   whose heart
is quieter than sand.   Here is the woman I love   whose heart

is quieter than steam in a jar, whose heart threatens
like a ripe fig, whose heart is a rag   red

as mulberries. Here is the woman I love
and the path that she took, whose footprints folded like an ironed shirt,

whose toes trailed gently in the wet stones,   whose path
is like water,   whose path is wrinkled

like a distance is wrinkled by heat. If she is like the earth,
she is like the earth

and shall move under you   like the earth. If she cried out
in a language you do not understand,

you will cry out   in a language you will not
understand.   The heart of Africa beats

in Africa   but her shadows lengthen
like a tide in London,   her face

folds like a brain in Paris,   her skin bellows
like a pocket in Lisbon,   her hair

unravels like water in Brussels,   her sinews tighten
like burnt plastic in Washington.   She lives

in a concrete house brittle as a jar   with nothing but her flesh
and a red dress,

and the whistling staves   of the telephone wires.
God bless those whose brilliance is obscured

by violence, God bless   the impotently good.
Today is as bright and chilly as gold,   as yellow

as a mowed field of maize,   but remember
the quarry scraped grey   as rubber filings, and remember

the waterhole tiled   with heat, and the dancing bees,
and remember remembering

like travelling backwards in a train,   and remember the quiet soil
outlives the maize.

Goud Rivier

This black river   must take me to the sea.
I row along it like a crack.   It breaks at my keel like lettuce leaves.

The river is as true as television
making me believe in things that do not exist.

I observe a cow on the bank closely   and want to run my fingers
through its breath.

When I am at the sea   I will not want to go back
but will want to fill it with my tears   feeling it is my home.

The sea opens up   like the smell of baking,
but it is not the sea itself.
The reeds sway like tinsel.

The paddle-blade carves the water into knots. Drops come off like a spoor.
The sound of the sea starts edging in.
The wind is in my muscles.

The water turns to gold and the river takes its name.

The river opens blindly   it does not reach the sea.
I pull the boat onto the sand spit   that stops its mouth.
My shadow says

I am a man with a paddle pulling a boat onto the sand.
I am not a boy. I own this.

I approach the turquoise sea   its ends fluttering like washing.

My shadow falls behind me   the colour of sand.

I find a perfect red stone that is a seed,
feathers
and the cuneiform of birds' feet

between the sea   and a gold river,
this river that brings me nothing   but a stone.

I must take it back to see what grows.
There it will be my home.

Rhapsody

Say that a fire advances up a match
like a fluorescent tide recalls the harbour as Lusaka shines at night.
          That a match

bends after the fire like a swan's neck a small death.
That its sharp head shines

like a stone. That here we could start anywhere
and arrive.

Say that the windows
gape like exit wounds. That the bone-white pillars unfasten

in tentacles, slipping in and out of stone. That every point unleashes
a dancing alphabet. That the longing eyes in the tiles

are like beans. That in Dakar the Arab clerics
knew a mystery.

Say that shafts of gold burst through the saints and virgins.
That the injured children's brown tears

are like melting flesh. That on the floor's map
flow the ants in rifts. That a penny-whistle threads the colonnades

of Maputo. That all we are holding
wants to let go.

Say that we don't know
what we know and aren't what we seem. That the physical forms

are eliding with the words and the rhymes
are rhyming internally.

That all we are holding wants to let go.
That here we could start anywhere and arrive.

Steel Mill

Smudge
at a distance:

wake
of a banking ship turning;

malleable plume,
vulnerable to the wind,

Nike tick,
insubstantial *yes* to existence,

floss-thin arc
to which all things go,

columns
felled

by the gentlest of movements.

Though vital enough
in the dark;

miraculous
and all-sufficient,

as a god,
who once appeared nightly

like this:

a viscous flare,
dancing hands

or cloth
(a rolling flag of light),

depthless imposition on space,

jagged neon breath,
floodlit silk,

oily exclamation mark.

San Tomé

In San Tomé
the fishing boats loll in the sand

with their keels falling open
like gashed yellow pods.

The balconies are the white
of cuttlefish spines

and the bellowing walls
are the green of lime

and the blue is the blue
of a clipped sapphire sea

that its scraped out coasts
have never seen

and the palms dust the air with their fronds.

In San Tomé there's a lady standing
in cotton and pearls

who has slippered
her feet in the cusp of the bay

and is up to her ankles
in honey and gold.

How my heart would let her
lift me away

when the sifting breeze
has blown her feet free

and the setting sun
has set just enough

since I know she can sing
and want her to sing just for me.

Banknote

Your elaborate mosaics and stately patterns and intricate structural
                                                            formations
and diabolical colour gradients,
a scaly star, a tree filled with diamonds and other substances defying
                                                            replication,
your rose-windows and curls, your grand stars, fists, wreathes and
                                                            inscriptions,
your cocoa, wood and gold, your humble ships at port,
ochre-stained and water-stained,
miraculous token of trust related to nothing tangible,
proof of society since the emptying of the gold-merchant's cellar.

The Accident

Your forehead bleeds silk handkerchiefs,
your hair falls apart like a husk of grain.
Now your dancing tendons are snapped,
your neck broken like a clip;
your lips play at lazy angels in the sand
and leaves brush your ear's soft conch.
Cold flows into your bones like diamonds.
Your tumble plucked the country fence like a lute.
With feeling curl and tremble the tendrils of wire
– attentive foliage. Vines embroidered your fall.
What a set piece is this:
A clump of spider-nettles grows from the rusks of your hand;
beneath your head, your number plate furls.
Bunny-eyed you lie in your headlight's lime
(tomorrow it will bleach you to salt),
mildly surprised by your fate, the future.
Too late (the legend goes), you missed the sign
(now its all detail: fine as a petal scored with verses,
the grain of the post flowing like a zebra's pelt).
Stylish was the death of this bourgeois:
the content of him spills back into the ground,
this lord of the land, this commander in chief.

'These jewels'

These jewels
stones of the earth

smell ever more of home   in exile
from imagined homes,

where a sea slaps a city
and aqueducts cross the veld   scandalising the baobabs.

However   it is not enough that somewhere else everything is possible.

Water here
flows principally in sheets

and rarely carves out streams.

There is no purchase
on the land   there is no general home.

When next again the doors swell gently in their frames
imagine this:

a million windows
swivelling round each glassy bead

a spring   knitting a fountain

a treadmill of possibilities,

work and play

work and play.

Pastoral

I'm tired of this pretty love. I'm tired of this anaesthetic love,

fresh as a sapphire,
numb as formaldehyde,

tired
of the wind
slipping under the skin
lifting muscle
from bone,
sending the senses back up the paths of the world to the flesh,

of the rapids of fruit,
of the hedgerows of wheat
cropped like a boy's fringe,
of the mulberries falling like beads,

of sand's apathy,
of light's apathy,
spilling like the static of insects,

of the conjuring tricks of daring rock,
of cloud's acrobatics on Signal Hill,
of the grains of glass carpeting
the bay,
of the island's thin-lipped acquiescence
in the bay,

I'm tired.

Earth is now given notice to burn with my version of history:

Stone wall, play back the scenes you absorbed,
mountains, give back the bones that you hoard.
Shuffle your images, sea.
Plough, be a stylus playing the land,
catch the splinter of steel on an old battlefield.
Fine sand, skid at the feet,
fine sand, scour the grain of the feet,
drill the trunk;
iron, fray like paper,
well and unfurl like swollen wood,
wave, have your force skimmed from your face,
wave, shed yourself like entry into the earth's atmosphere,
burn like a shield of fire,
fizz like a tablet,
thrash and harry the shore like you want it all back, and aren't going to
                                                            go easily

because this is how people forget:

as ice melts,
releasing its tares,
as water glosses the rent in a stone.

The Boy

The boy who runs away from everything runs.
He wears his class uniform. His costume is traditional,
his tie flaps on his flat belly like a dog's pink tongue.
He wraps himself in a blanket from all people.
The skin of his dreams smells like wood fires.
He watches the people in overalls. Where do *they* drink,
where do their hearts drink?
Why won't he ever be home?

'Let your sailing ships'

Let your sailing ships
rot quietly   in their emerald bays,

let their leaking holds spill beads   into the sea;

let the tracking-dogs
turn wild,

let the beaters
turn keen gardeners,

and the delta's
belle chose

be undefined.

Leave aside the primer,
leave the Bible,

and the looting of several small places
for others to endure.

Our heroes can stay ordinary.

Tell them
history has no future here

there's nothing here to find   except the weather

and the landscape,
that the cow's milk comes out sour,

and the honey isn't pure

and there's very little water
and not a trace of gold.

Let us cope without your patronage
and live

without your law

and watch
the evening stealing twilight

through the windows
and grow old.

Last Drive

Dipping into the gutter of valleys came the terribly gentle pall
above the burnt veld, changing season and hemisphere, a softening,
                                        scentless mist of particles
lifting the earth, a cataract over the windshield dulling the senses, a
                                                   landscape
as desolate as the European cold
and patches of earth jet-black as a slick (imagine, from a height, the
                                            countryside rolling
like a dalmatian's back);

then opening-up amphitheatre of building, tenements illuminated like
                                                burning bookends,
flyovers whisking past like the underside of a centipede;
peri-urban fringe –
radio mast, garage, the ribcage of distant hills, the pace of steel girders
                                                   heart-beating time,
the poetry of repetition – more like acid than the edge of a blade,
and I recall
how roadside flames licked up like wild grass in time-lapse,
those jumping slippery shapes now too far outside human time to catch.

'Throw your arms up as if you'd pluck bullets from the air'

Throw your arms up as if you'd pluck bullets from the air,
as if they'd fly from the barrel
into your palms like pigeons.

Your waiting coffin shines like a box of light,
your life will spill into the sand like a knotted scarf.

x

They come to the village and smash the mothers
and twist the horses –
these machines,
soldiers, no wonder some dream of their wicked buckles,
and their balls packed tight as lettuces.

x

The skull in the ash like a bubble of milk?
(I wasn't there),

and the fingers sprouting like beans?
(I wasn't there),

and the insects unknitting the flesh, and the teeth
like a packet of seeds?

x

You come to me,

give me my white shirt,
give me my coffin of light,
you hold out my arms in the air.

The birds puff out in lazy formations
that won't even come to me.
One sits on the officer's cap that looks like a bucket.
I grow tired.
I ask permission to sit down on the ground.
The officer goes home to brush his moustaches.
The others drift away to their wives' cooking.
I play with a feather in the sand.
By the light of my coffin I gather my scarf,
I smooth my lapels
I get up and go.

Tomorrow we do this again.

x

You're cement flowing under my hands, you're space folded out
in flowing stone,
you're holes,
you're my Pompeii.
This is my proof —
I could not have been there.

x

I'm sitting in the dust when a shadow falls across me,
and I split like a stone,
the one half in the light listening, the other holding itself in its hands,
its head as dense as a planet.

By morning the news is out:
Its raining birds like nails.

Celeste

We are the lions in this kingdom, sang the Liberian
in the steel cafe made of a container
at the bus station, to himself –
            but he wasn't,
and he went and asked a white man
for a cigarette and money

and got neither. Further on was nothing but sand and wood
and the suffering of animals doing
man's work,
being paid with a whip.

The guide went ahead,
beating a harnessed cow with a stick – the cow that carried our food.
The sand wanted to stop my feet.

The man in the compound we leave
carries on stalking around. He fucks all the women in this town –
all the pregnant girls are his.
Once there was an empire here, somewhere there still is,
but I can't see it.
I'm just a white man

today. The stairs to the citadel flower
with tobacco.
The bones of the city are filled with stones and birds
and the sounds of the valley towns. Today your capital is just a village,
adequate and efficiently organised.
In my weakness

I believed only in what I could see,
I cared only for you –
Celeste – who gave yourself to a stranger,
whose name was taken down   from the stars by men chancing their lives
on the sea for money.
I don't recall

what its like to feel   what I thought I had learned
though I remember the words

which are all that remain:

give yourself as a gift,
        you said,
        and you'll learn to love again.

'Maybe you don't have to know why'

Maybe you don't have to know why,
you must just admit,

since the heart's fist
will not always unclench.

Maybe you don't have to know why,
you must just admit,

since the seams were too deep
in your anatomy for reason,

there was poison already
in the ventricles.

Maybe you don't have to know why,
you must just admit.

You must say what you saw:
the rising wings of your own collarbones,

and the sails of your chest,
and your flimsy veins wrinkling with blood

and that life is a physical thing.

Maybe you don't have to know why,
you must just admit.

Maybe you just have to say:

I cannot bear to hate my enemies;
that only their suffering made them perfect;
and you're most alone when you're with them.

Maybe you don't have to know why,
you must just admit

and outside the courts
the women will gather the silent child on their backs
and take him through the streets,
and put him to sleep with the scent of soap and the sweat in their clothes,
and with singing dissolve the stones in his throat,
and return him to his own mother.

'The children began flying up to their houses'

The children began flying up to their houses,
past the family's washing on the stairs,
small children flying on their dresses,   they were birds flying.
Everyone came out in their pyjamas to sing,
a baby ran past a motorcycle's spinning wheel.
The dust lay thick on the kitchen shelves,
the well was dry to its floor,
at which point I noticed the aerials,   like needles threading the moon,
and that all the people had become strangely, joyfully transparent,
those who were living   and the dead alike.

Oshogbo

A little way on   the forest was bringing itself down tree by tree
the bark was unpeeling itself   cracking in the air
and the spirits were pouring out of the roots   and the birds were
                                          rustling and clicking.

The stone gods grew from the roots,   flat stone women
whose fingers exploded like bananas,
whose breasts were like pointed desert fruit.
Around them the vines of the forest coiled,   hissing like electricity cables.

Suddenly a river came round the bend,   pulling pieces of light down
                                          its way;
the monkeys began praying to the river.
We were in the widest, coolest place, where the skies were growing
and falling away,   the forest was moving.
I put my forehead on the foot of the god and the cool forest jumped
                                          into me,
and the birds turned madly like rusted gates.

Further on   the river came round again to cut us off   but the banks
                                          sprung a bridge
and the hair of the river twisted away around the rocks.
You be no man   came the forest in me,
You now be no man,
and the river flipped a curl up the bank and tapped my ankle
Now you be no man-o!

Me, I Will Be With You

★

Humbly I appear at the gates of your city,

                                               a cat in a doorway.

I am inclusive of all the protagonists.
I wear feathers like a conquistador.
I bear gifts.
I am the gift itself.
I have come to steal your souls in a box.

★

Find the shards of my crockery, the brittle blue veins of my diet
      in your sedimentary rocks,

find my delicate metalwork holding out like sand, and my elaborate threads
      unpickable in your clothes.

Learn to be sensitive of similarities. Mistrust your inquisitiveness now.
Bring me shackled to your courts.
Kill me while you can.

*

I will lie around you like sleep. I will be as hills folding
                into the sea.

Never leaving you, I will enfold you as you wake.
You being to me like a bay,
I will sail in the palm of your hand.

I will be your horizon.
I will whisper in your ear.
I will be the medium of your thoughts.

★

The laden quays,
the dew turning steel into dust on the empty quays,
the carriages clicking like coins,
the steel threads lacing the sleepers in their beds of weed,
the powerplant's living brambles,
the comfortless glitter of candlelight,
the scaffolds and the lecterns
will all be me,

me in the hoe,
me in the liturgy of the branch-meeting,
me in the commodity price,
at the waterhole   me.

In the forts the breakers sounding through the high turrets of light,
in the vaulted rooms
        recalling a medieval college,
in the cloisters,
in the libraries stacked tight as slave ships,
in the cool dank thick-walled rooms suggesting
        a comfortable villa,
in the cellars of vats,
in the furtive headlands,
        in the slap of clothes wrung on the rocks,
it will be me,

me in the shipping-ways,
me in the oceans pitted like pincushions,
me in the veins of sap scraped in the jet-streams,

        me in the water of your skin –

★

which, waking,
    you will find has been turned into salt by the stars,

and inexplicably you will grow silent
and abandon the room,
and be heard of rattling the fences in the town, and smashing the beads
                                                                    of light
in the town;
and be furious and full of desire,
and discover the colour of your love,

and be recovered
but I will never forgive your absence,

and never understand myself,
listening at night to the stars falling and falling
like the memory of salt,
and grow old hating my powers, and let the gardens weep
with their ruin,
and sleep with the door unlatched,

and sing softly
'come home' –
mayibuye.

Five Versions of Leaving and Being Left

1 'I sold you'

I sold you for a kerosene flame   distended like a tongue
in Kampala.

I gave you away for a broken city on a hill   filled with my people.

I left you for passing conversations with strangers who persist in believing
      and with whom I will probably be defeated.

I left you for a language that rolls in the mouth like pebbles   and is
                        heard singing
      in the hills you can't see   from the road,

      while yours is not.

I left you because there is nothing so momentarily sufficient   as the
                        fireflies
      bursting like pollen
      along a winding path.

I lost you because you took the side of everything I was trying to outwit
                and evade

but also because I wouldn't want you to think I was easy.

I lost you because when I staggered up the hill, fearing
                for my life,   stopping
      to lean on my knees   and recover
      all there was at the top of the hill   was another hill,

      not you;

because when I tore like dough   I found your hands on only one side,

to give myself to something possibly sham because I believed it,

because when the water table finally rose   it came up through the soles
                of my feet.

2 'The fruit lies out in broken rows'

The fruit lies out in broken rows,
its gold buttons spilling.

The soft fruit throbs under my thumbs,

its muscular chambers lie open,
each an aorta packed with glistening seeds.

3 The Last Thing

When I drove and I drove and I drove to Knysna   and the shacks were
                                                 falling down the hills
to the sea   and the road opened like light

adhering to the edges of a brass bell
and the dark hills lined up   like wise men

and the distances tore past under my feet   and then I could not bear
its tearing

the last thing I felt was your touch,
like pale blind fish in a cave   but that will pass.

When my ribs opened   like two red fans
and my breath   came out like rivers, and caught on the stones
           and spilled

and all I heard   was the stars marrying with the pale grass
(it was the sound of a hundred falling   silver leaves)

and I was gathered up in a blanket of sand

the last thing I saw was your face, white as the moon
but that will pass.

When the sky folded away my affairs,
and I slipped from my skin   as from a shining wrapper

and I lay above myself like smoke above a veld   as well as like muddy
                                                     water
and I no longer had a body

the last thing I knew   was your body
like a snake wrapped in its tissue skin

but that will pass.

And when the bushes and stones pecked at me
and I thinned   like honeycomb

and the last thing I felt on my skull were your cheeks,
soft   as dust in a soft wind

and you whispered to me again
and again

and the last thing I heard   were the ants crawling in my head

and the grass and the trees drew me up
and the stone of me   opened up like a bean

and I pushed into the air   as if tying many knots through it
and then I was in the air

all the names I called first
were your names

but that will pass.

4 *Walking to Antarctica*

The heat
bleaches the moon to its bones.

The bay shines dully
like steel.

A harbour lies beneath the sill,
the customs-house

red as muscle,
the cranes with their delicate necks

their tendons
supple as bath-chains.

Stamping the air with their Braille
the foghorns call –

the tankers wait

tethered and laden
and blind as egg-white

but with you   in this bed I'm as safe as asylum

free
to love you as much as I like.

★

Inside you, sleeping,
like moths beneath your lids

pictures stir.
Soon they will wake,

shedding dust,

opening out into thought,

and turning
you'll say

*Addie, if the sea
emptied out, would we go for a walk?*

★

I travel far above you,
reporting

through distances as deep as space
a terrain as remote
         as a distant moon.

I see your rare face,

its aspect turning:

today you have just arrived
but already I know

now is the beginning
of the last time I see you.

5 Oxford

Fulfilling an obligation I creep along.
The cold scalds my chin.
My warm teeth are pearls.
My eyes are like crystal.
Water brings a lurching, deceptively uncontrollable loneliness.

This Is What It's Like to Feel

1 'A dazzling light invades the eye'

A dazzling light invades the eye.
This is what its like to feel:
Sea lifted along its ribs; scales catching, full of its own life,
its softness from afar, its actual grittiness, is constant willingness
to make you out with touch.
Echoes of colour awaken themselves,
rearranging the way I am.
They hum along the circuits of my whirling thumbs.
I comb it with my hands
in which the slow fish are fiercely alive, whose distant movement
adheres to the skin
like a wind bearing silk. The world is such a vast individual
with whom I am in constant contact,
as radio waves encircle the flesh,
as news enters the bone,
as the blood brings information
with which the muscles ache.

2 'A car swivels past, going from ear to ear'

A car swivels past, going from ear to ear,
and unfolds its shape and throbs with sound.
A waiter slices the pavement in half, cutlery spluttering
like a fuse.
The blades of his shoes snip too
like the scrape of a struck match. His buttons
blast through him with light.
Distantly, the voices of children swim in and out of tune
unravelling and winding back into plaits of sound.
That's how it is,
such little dramas of sensation.
As for what the camera saw
I couldn't say.

3 'I breathe my ragged cartoon diamond breath'

I breathe my ragged cartoon diamond breath.
Even the air is thin matter, a consommé of specks.
The seething body fills the skin.

I cannot imagine empty space,
nor the boundaries of myself.

4 'An old man's porous face'

An old man's porous face –
                    I saw him
and moved through the air where his head had been.
A stuck door snapped open like a wrist, slithers of heat
shearing the air.
The beautiful French ride by on the brush-strokes
of their scarves.
The orange crabs beg, glistening,
the ragged clams keep out a soft grey ear,
oysters spit a sour pearl.
The crowd effervesces.
Flat streaking leaves pat the air.
The draining sky hurtled invisibly into my face. (I'd scream
                              if I didn't know it).
The metro smells of nuts and brings music from stop to stop.
Its ways are mysterious, its dark careful weaving
must spell a dance.
The cheeks of the poor are hollow everywhere.
For such small amounts they sing,
singing all along the mysterious, winding ways.

5 Still Life

The continent's weight overflows the bay, the weather leans
into the cape.
The cool flesh braces itself, the harness of the skin simmers,
and the pores mine the flesh.

The air enfolds the body in its creases of sound.
The sights of the world flood the pupil,
saturate the jelly of the eye,
stain the flesh,
like radiation   encode the blood.

The mind scintillates with the presence
of the world,
sprawls in the hammock of its nerves.

The world holds me closely,

by the metronome of the blood   holds
my lifetime steady.